THE **FESTIVE** FOOD OF
Thailand

BY JACKI PASSMORE

photography by
Will Heap

Kyle Cathie Limited

This edition first published in Great Britain 2006 by
Kyle Cathie Limited
122 Arlington Road
London NW1 7HP
general.enquiries@kyle-cathie.com
www.kylecathie.com

Originally published 1992

ISBN 1 85626 632 X
ISBN (13-digit) 978 1 85626 632 1

Previous page: Richard Nebesky/Robert Harding World Imagery/
Getty Images
This page: Istock images

Designed by **pinkstripedesign.com**

Photography by **Will Heap**

Illustrations by **Sally Maltby**

Home economy by **Annie Nichols**

Styling by **Roisin Nield**

Production by **Sha Huxtable & Alice Holloway**

Reproduction by Image Scanhouse
Printed and bound in China by SNP Leefung Printers Limited

CONTENTS

SAWASDEE PIMAI

The Thais celebrate their New Year on April 13 with boisterous festivities focused on water splashing. But they also acknowledge the Christian New Year and Chinese Lunar New Year, consuming vast quantities of the sort of foods that promise longevity and extended happiness: fried and soft noodles, soup noodles, sweet and sour crisp noodles they call Mee Krob and the dish they inherited from the Portuguese traders of the 16th century, *Foi tong*, threads of gold.

left Dai villagers celebrate New Year, Guang Niu/Reportage/Getty Images

MEE KROB

CRISP NOODLES

Mee Krob is also popular as an offering to the monks during Buddhist Lent. Their sweet, tart flavour and inviting crunch make a delight as a first course. The crisp red noodles look particularly festive mounded high on one of the blue and white footed dishes that the Thais use for serving.

170g fine rice noodles
(vermicelli)
oil for deep-frying
2 eggs, well beaten
2 large dried Chinese black
  mushrooms, soaked in water
30g dried shrimps, soaked
4 garlic cloves, chopped
1 small onion, chopped
1 fresh red chilli, seeded
  and chopped
170g chicken breast, cut into
  fine shreds
50g firm bean curd, cut into
  fine shreds
2 tablespoons light soy or fish
  sauce (nam pla)
2 tablespoons rice or
  mild vinegar
juice of 1 lime
2 tablespoons tomato ketchup
85g palm or (dark) brown sugar
shredded fresh red chilli
fresh beansprouts to garnish
chives to garnish
fresh coriander to garnish

serves 6–8

1 Divide the rice noodles into small bundles. Heat the oil in a large pan or wok until quite hot. (If the oil is not hot enough the noodles will toughen and not expand.) Fry the noodles in batches for just a few seconds on each side until well puffed. Remove immediately before they begin to colour. Pour the oil from the pan (and reserve) and wipe out.

2 Add the eggs, moving the pan slowly over the heat so they set in a thin film. Cook lightly, flip and cook the other side, then remove and leave to cool. Squeeze the water from the mushrooms, remove the stems and cut the caps into fine shreds. Drain and chop the shrimps.

3 Return 3 tablespoons oil to the pan and fry the garlic and onion until golden. Add the chilli and chicken and cook until the chicken changes colour, then add the mushrooms, shrimps and bean curd, and cook briefly. Remove from the pan.

4 Mix the soy or fish sauce with the rice vinegar, lime juice, tomato ketchup and sugar, stirring well. Pour into the pan and simmer, stirring, until syrupy.

5 Add the noodles and keep them moving in the pan until evenly coated with the syrup. Quickly return the cooked ingredients, except the egg, and stir evenly. Cook just long enough to heat through, then mound on a serving dish. Roll the egg crêpe and cut crossways into fine shreds. Scatter the egg and chilli over the top of the noodles and decorate with the beansprouts, chives and coriander. Serve at once.

NOODLES IN CURRY SAUCE

For best results, use uncooked king prawns in their shells. Sold headless, they are 8–10cm long, and you should get 18–20 prawns per 450g.

700ml thin coconut milk
  (extract)
4 garlic cloves, chopped
3 large spring onions,
  chopped (greens separated)
2 white root ends of lemongrass
  stalks, halved lengthways
5 thick slices fresh ginger root,
  shredded
1 tablespoon shrimp paste (*kapi*)
1 tablespoon palm or
  (dark) brown sugar
salt and/or fish sauce (*nam pla*)
350g diced chicken meat
12 medium peeled uncooked
  prawns
500ml thick coconut milk
  (cream)
250g dried rice noodles
  (vermicelli)
1 red and 1 green chilli, deseeded
  and finely shredded
100g fresh beansprouts,
  blanched
1 small bunch sweet basil
3 hard-boiled eggs
lime wedges

serves 6

1 Pour the coconut milk into a saucepan and bring almost to the boil, stirring slowly. Add the garlic, white parts of spring onion, lemon grass, ginger, shrimp paste and sugar and simmer for about 20 minutes until the flavours are well established and the coconut milk slightly reduced.

2 Add salt and/or fish sauce to taste, the chicken and shrimps (deveined as on page 89) with the thick coconut milk and simmer for a further 10 minutes or until the chicken is tender.

3 Meanwhile drop the noodles into a pan of boiling water to soften; drain well. Transfer to a serving dish. Scatter the chillies, beansprouts and basil leaves over the noodles. Pour on the sauce.

4 Cut the eggs into wedges or thick slices and arrange on the noodles with wedges of lime. Sprinkle over the green parts of the spring onions and serve.

GOLDEN THREADS

Portuguese traders arriving in Thailand in the 16th century brought their recipes for *fios de ovos* or egg threads, a delicate dish of fine strands of egg simmered in a sugar syrup said to have been created by nuns centuries earlier. Thai aristocracy, impressed by its alternative name, *ovos reais* or royal eggs, requested it on banquet menus. The 'threads of gold' are wrapped into little cushions and piled into a pyramid called a *wai*.

6 duck and 6 chicken eggs,
  at room temperature
800g fine white sugar
350ml water
a few drops of jasmine or
  rose essence

serves 6

1 Separate 6 duck and 5 chicken eggs, saving the whites for another use. Add the whole chicken egg and beat gently, then pass through a fine sieve.

2 In a wide saucepan bring the sugar and water to a slow boil and simmer until the syrup becomes slightly thick. Add the jasmine or rose essence.

3 Using a paper cone with a small hole at the end, or a piping bag with a fine nozzle, allow the egg to flow into the hot syrup in thin streams. When set, remove with chopsticks, winding them into bite-sized portions resembling little skeins of embroidery thread. Sprinkle a little boiling water into the syrup from time to time to prevent it becoming too thick. Thai cooks store the *foi tong* overnight in an airtight container with the fresh flowers to impart extra flavour and aroma. *Foi tong* are best done a day in advance.

Visaka Buja

The anniversary of the birth, enlightenment and passing into Nirvana of the Lord Buddha is celebrated in mid-May. It is the holiest day in the Thai calendar, with thousands of people thronging monastery courtyards, offering candles and flowers to the Buddha. Many temples are illuminated with thousands of paper lanterns.

left Thai devotees pray at a temple in front of a statue, Saeed Khan/AFP/Getty Images

FISH AND BEAN CAKES

A dish you will enjoy as much as the monks do.

8 shallots, peeled
3 garlic cloves, peeled
1 white root end of lemongrass
stalk, roughly chopped
1 green chilli, seeded
2cm piece fresh ginger root,
roughly chopped
2 teaspoons finely chopped
coriander root
2 teaspoons grated lime peel
1 teaspoon shrimp paste (*kapi*)
2 teaspoons salt
½ teaspoon ground black pepper
1 egg, beaten
170g long snake beans, sliced
vegetable oil
550g white fish fillets, skinned

makes about 24

1 In a mortar or food processor, grind the shallots, garlic, lemongrass and chilli to a paste, add ginger, coriander root, lime peel and shrimp paste and grind again. Add the seasonings and fish and process until smoothly blended, adding 3 tablespoons iced water and the egg to make the paste lighter. Stir in the sliced beans.

2 Heat 5cm oil in a wide, flat pan. Form the mixture into small balls and flatten into patties. Fry in the hot oil until golden, turning once. Drain well and serve warm with very finely sliced cucumber pickled in vinegar sweetened with sugar

MEB MANGLUK

BASIL SEEDS
IN SWEET COCONUT MILK

1 tablespoon dried seeds of
  sweet or lemon-scented basil
575ml thick coconut milk
  (cream)
palm or dark brown sugar
2 green coconuts (optional)
cracked ice

serves 4

1 Place the seeds in a small bowl, cover
with cold water and leave for several hours
until they soften and develop a gelatinous
coating. Drain.

2 Sweeten the coconut milk to taste with
sugar, divide between four glasses and add
the basil seeds.

3 Open the coconuts, pour off the water
and use a teaspoon to scrape out the soft
flesh; shred, add to the glasses with plenty
of ice and serve.

Nam Katee

NGAN WEI WAH

Astrologers decree the most auspicious time and date for a Thai wedding, even if it means beginning the elaborate ceremony in the mists of early morning. Festivities continue far into the night and the buffet table is constantly replenished with a plethora of savoury snacks and elegant sweetmeats.

Perhaps the most significant sweet is *kanom sam kloe* or 'three chums'. The batter-coated sweetmeats are fried in groups of three, and in some parts of Thailand in fours.

Optimistic parents and nervous brides watch as the sweetmeats turn golden in the oil. If they stick together, it augurs a full and happy marriage. If one departs company the marriage will be childless. A bleak future is in store for the couple if they all float off separately. Many a concerned relative has resorted to subterfuge, inserting toothpicks in the balls, or using a thick batter to ensure a promising result.

right Thai wedding ceremony, ML Sinibaldi/Corbis

KANOM SAM KLOE

THREE CHUMS

115g white or brown sugar
2 tablespoons palm (or [dark] brown) sugar
85g mung beans
75g white sesame seeds
125g glutinous rice flour
185g shredded coconut
oil for deep-frying

BATTER
170g rice flour
75g glutinous rice flour
large pinch of salt
1 large egg, beaten
250ml thin coconut milk (extract)

makes about 50 pieces
(serves 9-12)

1 In a small saucepan, mix the sugar and palm sugar with 100ml water. Bring to the boil and simmer for 10 minutes.

2 Heat a wok or small pan and slowly cook the mung beans, without oil, until they are well browned and very aromatic; transfer to a blender or mortar and grind to a powder. Pour into a mixing bowl. In the same pan brown the sesame seeds, stirring continuously. Mix with the mung bean powder and rice flour and the coconut. Pour the hot syrup over the dry ingredients and mix to a sticky mass.

3 In another bowl, make the batter by mixing the rice flour, glutinous rice flour and salt. Stir in the egg and half the coconut milk to form a smooth, thick batter, then add the remaining coconut milk.

4 Shape the filling into marble-sized balls, working with wet or lightly oiled hands if necessary. Heat the oil to moderately hot. Dip the balls into the batter three at a time and slide into the oil. Fry until golden and floating on the surface. Drain and serve, preferably while still warm.

PANAENG KRUANG DON

CHICKEN WITH RED CHILLI SAUCE

This is a winning centrepiece for a buffet.

5 chicken breasts, with skin
550ml thick coconut milk
6 dried red chillies
1–3 fresh red chillies,
   seeded
8 red shallots
4 garlic cloves
2½ pieces fresh ginger root
2–3 fresh coriander roots
1 white root end of
   lemongrass stalk,
   quartered

½ teaspoon shrimp paste (*kapi*)
3 tablespoons vegetable oil
salt and black pepper
soft brown sugar
soy or fish sauce (*nam pla*)
   to taste
lime juice and leaves
fresh coriander leaves

serves 6-12

1 Place the chicken breasts in a lightly greased oven dish, skin-side upwards, and bake for about 20 minutes at 190°C/380°F/gas 5 until tender. Set aside.

2 In a saucepan, simmer the coconut milk until well reduced; this will take at least 35 minutes. Soak the dried chillies in boiling water for 10 minutes, drain, cut open and deseed. Place in a mortar or food processor with the fresh chillies, shallots, garlic, ginger, coriander roots, lemongrass and shrimp paste and grind to a smooth thick paste. Fry in the oil until the mixture is well coloured and very aromatic. Pour in half the reduced coconut milk and boil gently until a film of red oil floats on the surface. Season to taste with salt, pepper, brown sugar, soy or fish sauce and lime juice.

3 Skin the chicken and cut crossways into fingers. Place each piece on a washed lime leaf and arrange on a platter. Spoon a little of the sauce and the remaining coconut milk over each and sprinkle on chopped coriander leaves. Decorate the platter with decoratively cut chillies and carrots if desired.

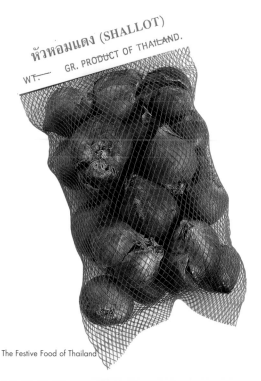

หัวหอมแดง (SHALLOT)
GR. PRODUCT OF THAILAND.
WT.

STICKY RICE WITH MANGO

The mango season begins in April so this dish is important in the marriage banquet during this and following months. The yellow skinned *ok-rong* mango is considered best for desserts.

450g glutinous rice
salt
450ml thick coconut milk
(cream)
55g crumbled palm or dark
brown sugar
4 ripe mangoes

serves 6

1 Rinse the rice well, then soak for at least 3 hours. Pour into a fine wire strainer or a colander. Place over simmering water to steam for about 50 minutes until tender.

2 Add a pinch of salt to the coconut milk and simmer gently in a small pan to thicken. Spoon off any oil that rises to the surface. Remove from the heat and leave to cool.

3 Dissolve the palm sugar in a small saucepan with a little water. Cool.

4 Spoon the rice into six oiled moulds, press in lightly to compress and smooth the top, then turn on to dessert plates. Peel and thinly slice the mango and arrange in a fan beside the rice. Pour on the cooled syrup and coconut milk.

PSURCH MONTKOL

The ploughing ceremony in mid-May is a traditional ritual performed before the royal family at the Pramane Ground in Bangkok to open the rice-planting season. Brahmin priests carry the Buddhist and Hindu images in a solemn procession and the central figure, Phya Rak Nah, the Lord of the Festival, is doubly honoured by being personally chosen by the King. Two white oxen draped in gold with red-clad attendants enter the ground, dragging the ceremonial plough. Rice seeds are scattered as the oxen plough and at the end onlookers eagerly scavenge for the rice to add to their own crops for good luck. The ritual predicts the growing conditions and the abundance of the next rice crop.

left Thai Brahmen plough using royal oxen during the annual royal ploughing ceremony in Bangkok, Pornchai Kittiwongsakul/AFP/Getty Images

KANOM FOY

FRIED MUNGBEAN CAKES

300g mung beans
350ml thick coconut milk
  (cream)
85g sugar
3–4 eggs, beaten

makes 24–30

1 Rinse the beans well and crack or crush them in a food processor. Leave to soak in cold water overnight.

2 Boil the soaked beans in the coconut milk in a closed pan until soft; drain, add the sugar and cook over very low heat until the mixture is thick and leaves the side of the pan cool. Shape into little balls. Dip into beaten egg and fry until golden.

JACKFRUIT SEEDS

This dish is named after jackfruit seeds as the croquettes end up the size of the seeds.

Prepare the mung beans as for *kanom foy* above, and form into little croquettes. Make a sugar syrup with 500g sugar and 350ml water. Simmer the croquettes in the sweet syrup until they float to the surface. Cool before serving.

CHICKEN AND CHILLI WITH BASIL

350g boneless, skinned
   chicken breasts
3 tablespoons vegetable oil
1 teaspoon sesame oil (optional)
3 spring onions, chopped
30g hot 'bird's eye' chillies,
   or 2–3 green chillies, seeded
   and chopped
40g loosely packed sweet
   basil leaves
2½ tablespoons fish sauce
   (*nam pla*)
1 teaspoon sugar
salt and pepper
1 teaspoon coriander
   seeds, toasted
lettuce leaves to serve

serves 4

1 Cut the chicken into very small cubes and sauté in the oil until it is very lightly cooked; remove and keep warm.

2 Sauté the onions and chillies briefly. Return the meat, add the basil leaves (roughly chopped), the fish sauce, sugar, salt and pepper and cook briefly; remove from the heat.

3 Grind the coriander seeds to a fine powder. Line a serving plate with lettuce leaves, arrange the chicken on top and sprinkle on the coriander. Serve at once.

KHAO PANSA

The Buddhist Lent begins in July and most Thai men enter a *wat* for at least a week during the three months before Tod Kathin marks the end of the rainy season and brings yet another festival. During Lent the Thais make merit (*tum boon*) and offer food to the monks on their daily rounds carrying their silver food bowls.

right A Thai Buddhist pilgrim offers a bowl to a Buddhist monk, Sena Vidanagama/AFP/ Getty Images

GAENG PED GAI HED FANG

CHICKEN AND STRAW MUSHROOM CURRY

6 garlic cloves, peeled

1½ white root ends of lemongrass stalks, roughly chopped

1 medium onion, roughly chopped

6 dried red chillies, seeded

2½ cm piece fresh ginger root

½ teaspoons shrimp paste (*kapz*)

2 coriander plants

80ml vegetable oil

1 tablespoon toasted coriander seeds

½ teaspoon freshly grated nutmeg

1½ teaspoons salt

800g boneless, skinned chicken, cubed

275g fresh or canned straw mushrooms, rinsed

3 kaffir lime leaves

350ml thin coconut milk (extract)

175ml thick coconut milk (cream)

serves 4-6

1 In a food processor or mortar, grind the garlic, lemongrass, onion, chillies, ginger, shrimp paste, and the roots and stems of coriander (reserving the leaves) into a thick paste. Fry gently in the oil for about 20 minutes.

2 Grind the coriander seeds to a powder, mix in the nutmeg and salt, stir into the fried paste and cook briefly. Add the chicken, mushrooms and lime leaves with the thin coconut milk and simmer for about 15 minutes. Add the thick coconut milk and the coriander leaves. Heat for 5–6 minutes, check the seasoning and serve over rice.

NGAN KAENG RER

In mid-October the Thais celebrate the end of the rains, and commemorate their Chinese ancestry with boat races. Slender rainbow-hued snake-like craft with proud dragon figureheads are threshed through the muddy Thai rivers under the power of a dozen oarsmen, to the screaming barracking of thousands of spectators amassed on the river banks.

left Rowers on two dragon boats, Tao Chuan Yeh/AFP/Getty Images
previous page Buddha statue overgrown by tree roots, Daryl Benson/ Getty Images

FRIED RICE

450g long grain white rice
625ml water
1½ teaspoons salt
1 medium onion, finely sliced
1–2 garlic cloves, chopped
1½ tablespoons vegetable oil
225g boneless, skinned chicken
   breast, cubed
2 large eggs, beaten
½ teaspoon black pepper
2 tablespoons fish sauce
   (*nam pla*)
170g tin crabmeat, drained

serves 6

1 Place the rice in a saucepan with a well fitting lid and heavy bottom. Add the water and salt, cover and bring to the boil. Reduce the heat to the very lowest setting and cook the rice without opening the pan for 15 minutes. Stir up the rice.

2 Meanwhile, briefly brown the onion and garlic in the oil. Add the cubed chicken and cook until it changes colour, then pour in the eggs and cook, stirring, until set. Add the mixture to the rice with the pepper, fish sauce and crabmeat, and stir thoroughly. Keep warm until ready to serve.

SWEET PORK

800g fresh bacon/pork belly
5 garlic cloves, crushed
3 tablespoons vegetable oil
2 tablespoons palm or dark
   brown sugar
1 tablespoon light soy sauce
2 tablespoons fish sauce
   (*nam pla*)

serves 4-6

1 Cut the pork into small cubes and place in a saucepan with the garlic and oil. Cook gently with the pan partially covered until the pork is tender – about 45 minutes. Sprinkle a little cold water on to the meat occasionally to keep it moist and prevent it sticking to the pan.

2 Add the sugar, soy and fish sauce to taste, giving the dish an equal emphasis on sweet and salty.

TOD KATHIN

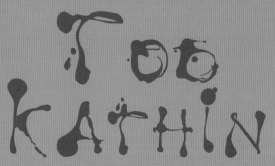

The Procession of the Golden Barges of the King to the
Monastery of the Dawn marks the end of Buddhist
Lent. The king travels on a colourfully adorned barge
to the temple, bringing with him gifts and new saffron-
coloured robes for the monks. The people form
processions to bring gifts to the monasteries all over
Thailand, many choosing to celebrate simultaneously
the end of the rainy season by trekking to country
wats, picnicking en route.

left Royal barges float down the Chao Phya River
in front of the Temple of the Emerald
Buddha,Stephen Jaffe/AFP/Getty Images

KA YAKU

GREEN RICE SOUP

Rural Thais look forward to November for a unique culinary treat, a creamy soup served sweet or salty made from green ears of young rice just before it begins to turn gold.

1kg young green rice ears with leaves (see tip below)
600–800ml water
6 pandanus (*toey*) leaves
sugar to taste

serves 4-6

1 Place the ears of rice and their leaves in a food processor with the water and pandanus leaves and grind to a thick paste. Pass through a fine sieve.

2 Gently heat the rice purée, adding sugar to taste. It will turn slightly transparent when done. Serve warm or cold with lightly salted thick coconut milk.

tip White rice can be used, adding the pandanus leaves or green food coloring and jasmine essence for fragrance. Pandanus leaves are available at specialist Thai shops.

right Istock Images

Ngan Chang Surin

The calendar of Thai festivals includes two elephant round-ups. The vital role the elephant once played in Thai life is vividly demonstrated in the November round-up in Surin Province. It began as a round-up of wild elephants, but is now a major tourist event with spectacular displays by hundreds of elephants and their *mahouts* (handlers). Though smaller, the Chaiyaphum round-up in January plays out the full drama of mock battles and demonstrations of strength and skill.

right Neil Emmerson/Robert Harding World Imagery/Getty Images

PORK SATE

800g pork leg meat
1 tablespoon coriander seeds
1 teaspoon cumin seeds
⅓ teaspoon fennel seeds
1 teaspoon laos powder
1½ teaspoons ground turmeric
2 tablespoons vegetable oil
175ml thick coconut milk
  (cream)
oiled bamboo skewers

PEANUT SAUCE:
1½ tablespoons coriander seeds
2 teaspoons cumin seeds
3 dried red chillies, seeded
1 medium onion, grated
3 garlic cloves, crushed
2½cm piece fresh ginger root,
  grated
1 tablespoon very finely chopped
  lemongrass stalks
½ teaspoon shrimp paste
3 tablespoons vegetable or
  coconut oil
125g crunchy peanut butter
375ml thick coconut milk
  (cream)
1 tablespoon brown sugar
2 tablespoons light soy or
  fish sauce (*nam pla*)
cucumber to serve

serves 4–8

left Henry King/
Photonica/Getty Images
overleaf Saeed
Khan/AFP/Getty Images

1 Cut the meat into thin slices, then into narrow strips. Thread in a wave formation on to the skewers and arrange in a flat dish.

2 Toast the coriander, cumin and fennel seeds in a dry pan until very aromatic, grind to a powder and add the laos and turmeric. Mix in the oil and coconut milk and pour over the sate. Cover with clingfilm and refrigerate for at least 4 hours.

3 To make the peanut sauce, dry-roast the coriander, cumin and red chillies as above and grind finely. Fry the onion, garlic, ginger, lemongrass and shrimp paste in the oil until well coloured. Add the ground spices, peanut butter and coconut milk and stir on medium heat until the sauce is thick and creamy. Add the brown sugar and fish or soy sauce.

4 Cook the sate over glowing charcoal or under a hot grill, turning frequently and basting with the marinade. Spread the sauce in shallow dishes. Arrange the sate on a platter surrounded by cubed or sliced cucumber and serve at once with the sauce. Note: Leftover sauce can be frozen.

The Festive Food of Thailand

KLUAY KAG TOO

BANANAS IN COCONUT BUTTER

BATTER
140g freshly grated or
115g desiccated coconut
175ml thick coconut milk
(cream)
55g rice flour
55g plain flour
1 teaspoon salt
1½ teaspoons baking powder

1 large egg
1½ tablespoons white or
brown sugar
100ml water

12 small, just-ripe bananas
vegetable oil for deep-frying

makes 12

1 If you are using desiccated coconut, soak it in the coconut milk to soften. Combine all the ingredients with enough of the water to make a thick batter. Set aside for 15 minutes.

2 Heat the oil until reasonably hot. Peel the bananas and dip into the batter to coat thickly. Lower carefully into the hot oil, several at a time, and fry until the batter is golden and crisp. Drain and serve.

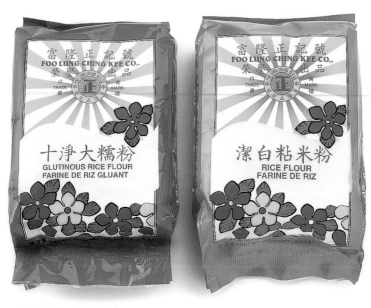

LOY KRATHONG

November 8 is Thailand's most picturesque festival. As the moon rises, thousands of boats made from paper or banana leaves are floated in the rivers, lakes and canals to pay homage to the Mother of Waters. Each tiny float is an art form in miniature of lotus blossoms, mythical animals and birds or symbolic beasts. Each carries a lighted candle, a stick of incense, flowers and a coin. The Thais believe that if the frail craft sail off without sinking or becoming entangled in the waterweeds their wishes will be granted and a prosperous future ensured.

left Loy Krathong festival at Wat Mahathat, ML Sinibaldi/Corbis

FAT HORSES

2 garlic cloves, peeled
2 coriander roots
5cm white part of
  spring onion
140g fat pork
75g chicken meat
75g raw prawn meat or
  170g tin crabmeat
3 tablespoons thick
  coconut milk (cream)
3 egg whites

1 tablespoon fish sauce
  (*nam pla*)
1 teaspoon soft brown
  or palm sugar
½ teaspoon cracked
  black pepper
fresh coriander leaves
shredded red chilli
18 heatproof ramekins,
  greased

makes 18

1 Place all the ingredients except the coriander leaves and chilli in a food processor or blender and grind to a smooth puree. Spoon into the ramekins and decorate each with a coriander leaf and a shred of red chilli.

2 Set on a rack in a steamer to steam over gently simmering water until firm – about 15 minutes. Remove from the steamer and leave to cool. Upturn on to a serving plate. The Thais traditionally serve it on a square of rinsed banana leaf.

LAYERED RICE CONFECTIONS

170g white sugar
250ml boiling water
125g rice flour
2 tablespoons potato
  or tapioca flour
350ml thick coconut
  milk (cream)
1–2 teaspoons jasmine
  or rose essence
pink, green or blue
  food colourings

makes 24 pieces

1 In a small saucepan, boil the sugar and water for 5 minutes to make a syrup. Set aside to cool.

2 In a bowl, combine the flours and stir in the coconut milk and warm syrup. Mix to a smooth batter. Divide into three or four portions. Leave one white and colour the other two or three, each with an individual colour.

3 Lightly oil an 18cm cake tin and place on a rack in a steamer over gently simmering water. Pour in a thin layer of white batter and steam, covered, until set – about 2 minutes. Pour over the first layer a thin layer of coloured batter, and steam in the same way until set. Continue until all of the batter has been used up and the cake is cooked. Allow to cool in the tin. Cut into diamonds, or use vegetable cutters to make the cake into fancy shapes. Serve cold.

FISH WITH GINGER SAUCE

1kg whole fish
  (snapper, bream, sea bass)
salt and white pepper
cornflour
oil for deep-frying
6 dried Chinese black
  mushrooms, soaked
3 tablespoons mild or
  rice vinegar
85g palm or brown sugar
75ml water
1 tablespoon sweet thick
  soy sauce
1 tablespoon fish sauce (*nam pla*)
100g young fresh ginger root,
  finely shredded
3 teaspoons cornflour
fresh coriander leaves to garnish

serves 4–6

1 Scale and clean the fish, rinse well and dry. Make several deep slashes across each side with a sharp knife. Season inside and out with salt and pepper. Coat the fish lightly with cornflour. Heat a little oil in a large frying pan, slide in the fish and cook to a deep golden brown. Turn carefully, using two large spatulas and cook the other side, then lift on to a serving platter and keep warm.

2 Drain the mushrooms, discard the stems and shred the caps. Set aside. In a small saucepan combine the vinegar, sugar and water. Simmer for 5 minutes until the sugar dissolves. Add the soy and fish sauces and the ginger and simmer for 6–7 minutes. Add the mushrooms and cook for a further 2–3 minutes. Mix the cornflour with a little cold water, pour into the sauce and stir on a low heat until thickened.

3 Pour the sauce at once over the fish and top with some coriander leaves.

NGAN ROM BOSANG

Paper umbrella-making is an important industry in northern Thailand. In January, in Chiang Mai, thousands of artisans celebrate their craft at the Umbrella Fair with parades and displays of their finest work in myriad colours and esoteric designs. The flower festival of Chiang Mai is also a spectacular event, with a procession of enormous floats encrusted with fresh flowers.

left Umbrellas, Chang Mai, Angelo Cavalli/zefa/Corbis

CHARGRILLED CHICKEN

A familiar sight at many outdoor festivals in northern Thailand is the itinerant vendor of grilled chicken. He sets up his portable charcoal grill, deftly secures a marinated chicken thigh in a triangle of bound bamboo twigs and grills it to nose-titillating succulence as you wait.

4 chicken thigh and
  drumstick pieces
3 garlic cloves
1¼ cm piece fresh ginger,
  roughly chopped
5cm piece lemongrass root,
  chopped
1 fresh coriander plant, leaves
  and roots, chopped
¾ teaspoon black peppercorns
1 tablespoon brown sugar
1 tablespoon fish sauce
  (*nam pla*)
2 teaspoons dark soy sauce
vegetable oil

serves 4

1 Use a sharp skewer to prick the chicken all over to allow the seasonings to penetrate, and to release fats. In a mortar or food processor grind the garlic, ginger and lemongrass reasonably smoothly, add the coriander and peppercorns and grind again. Mix with the sugar, fish sauce and soy sauce and spread evenly over the chicken. Allow to marinate for at least 1½ hours.

2 Place over glowing charcoal to cook for about 10 minutes, turning frequently, or roast in a preheated 220°C/425°F/gas 7 oven for about 40 minutes. Keep the chicken moist by brushing with any remaining marinade, and vegetable oil, during cooking. Serve in the fingers as a snack, or with rice and salad as a meal.

left Pornchai Kittiwongsakul/
AFP/Getty Images

Don Chedi

The Battle of Don Chedi in Suphan Bure is commemorated in January in high-spirited outdoor festivities and historical exhibitions. In 1592, King Naresuan the Great of Ayutthaya won a famous battle on elephant back against the leader of an enemy force, liberating the Kingdom of Thailand. In the 17th century, Ayutthaya was possibly the largest city in the world, with over a million inhabitants. Musaman Curry began auspiciously in Thailand, and continues to be a favourite at banquets. It was provided by the resident Muslim officials in Bangkok for a feast honouring King Rama I in the early 1800s. The curry sauce is of distinct Indian style, using the sweet spices of cinnamon, nutmeg, cardamoms and cloves rarely found in Chinese-inspired Thai cuisine.

right An elephant carries remains of Buddha, Reuters/Sukree Sukplang/Getty Images
previous page Paula Bronstein/Getty Images News

MUSAMAN CURRY

MUSLIM CURRY

Seven different fruits are used for this Double Seventh Festival recipe.

1 white root end of lemongrass
   stalk, quartered lengthways
2½ cm piece fresh ginger root
4 large garlic cloves, unpeeled
8 shallots, unpeeled
3 tablespoons vegetable oil
2 x 5cm cinnamon sticks
6 green (white) cardamom pods
2 bay leaves
2 teaspoons coriander seeds
4 dried red chillies, seeded
1 teaspoon shrimp paste (*kapi*)
½ teaspoon each of freshly grated
   nutmeg and ground mace
800g braising beef
575ml thin coconut milk
   (extract)
4 whole cloves
350ml thick coconut milk
   (cream)
400g cubed potato
8 small onions, peeled
   and left whole
125g roasted peanuts
salt
palm or brown sugar
lime juice or
   tamarind concentrate

serves 6-8

1 In a mortar or food processor, grind the lemongrass and ginger to a paste, then set aside. Fry the whole garlic cloves and shallots in the oil until very well browned, cool and then peel and mix the soft flesh with the lemongrass paste.

2 In a dry pan or wok, brown one of the cinnamon sticks, the cardamoms, bay leaves, coriander, chillies and shrimp paste until very aromatic. (Avoid the acrid fumes as you work!) Use a mortar or electric spice grinder to grind to a fine powder, add nutmeg and mace and set aside.

3 Cut the beef into cubes, place in a saucepan with the thin coconut milk, remaining cinnamon stick, cloves, and the lemongrass and ginger paste. Cover tightly, bring to the boil, and simmer for about 1¼ hours until the meat is tender. Remove the meat, add the spice powder, the thick coconut milk, potatoes, onions and peanuts and boil gently until the sauce is well reduced and richly flavoured. The vegetables should be tender-crisp. Season to taste with salt, sugar and lime juice or tamarind, return the meat and simmer gently for a few minutes. Serve with rice.

KANOM LUM FAO

COCONUT RICE SWEETS ON BANANA LEAF

Fao means to attend upon royalty; to serve sweets with this name would be considered a great compliment.

young banana leaf
100ml thick coconut milk (cream)
55g rice flour
30g glutinous rice flour
1 tablespoon mung bean
  or potato flour
115g sugar
350ml thin coconut milk (extract)
small pinch of salt
toasted sesame seeds

makes 24

1 Wipe the banana leaf with a clean cloth and cut out small rounds measuring about 5cm. Arrange on a tray.

2 In a small saucepan, slowly boil the thick coconut milk until it separates; remove the surface oil with a small spoon and continue to boil gently until the residue becomes quite thick.

3 In another saucepan mix the flours and sugar, stir in the thin coconut milk and salt and boil slowly, stirring continuously, until thick. Spoon a small portion of the thick batter on to each leaf, add a little of the thick cream and a few toasted sesame seeds and leave to set.

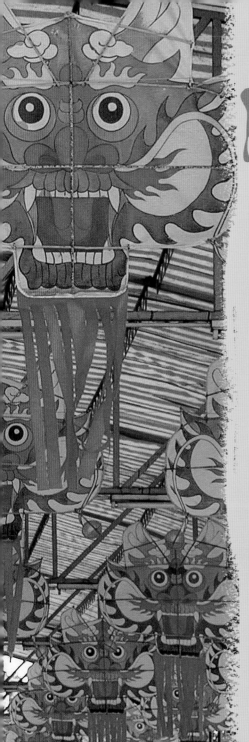

KAENG WAO

Kite flying is a popular sport in Thailand and the paper and bamboo kites are impressive examples of flight-engineering in spectacular designs. There are regular kite-flying competitions in Bangkok during March and April at the Pramane ground opposite the Grand Palace. Large 'male' kites or *chula*, oppose the smaller, more graceful 'female' kites, the *pakpao*. The kite-operating teams (for these are high-powered, enormous kites) manipulate the kites as they swoop and dive, the 'male' attempting to jag the 'female' with its barbs, she in turn dodging and weaving with the swift, sure movements of a dancer as she lures the 'male' to her airspace.

left Kites hanging up, Istock Images

GAENG TOM SOM

SWEET AND SOUR PORK RIB SOUP

700g meaty pork ribs
12 shallots, peeled
4 garlic cloves, peeled
2 teaspoons shrimp paste
  (*kapi*)
2 teaspoons salt
½ teaspoon ground black
  pepper
2 tablespoons vegetable oil
water
5cm piece fresh ginger root,
  shredded
40g shredded white or
  napa cabbage
60g sliced green beans
40g diced winter melon
  or chayote (*choko*)
1 tablespoon tamarind
  concentrate
palm or brown sugar
40g sliced bamboo shoots

serves 8

1 Use a heavy cleaver to cut the ribs into short pieces. Blanch in boiling water, drain and set aside, reserving the water.

2 In a mortar or food processor grind the shallots, garlic, shrimp paste, salt and pepper to a thick purée. Fry in the oil until very aromatic. Add the ribs and fry briefly, then add the water and the ginger. Bring to the boil, reduce the heat and simmer for 2 hours.

3 Skim the surface of the broth, add the cabbage, beans and melon and simmer until tender. Stir in the tamarind concentrate and sugar to taste, making it slightly tart. Add the bamboo shoots and serve.

pages 80-81 Don Klumpp/
Iconica/Getty Images

The Festive Food of Thailand

RED BEEF CURRY

8 dried red chillies, soaked in
  boiling water
3 dried kaffir lime leaves, soaked
  in boiling water
white root end of 1 lemongrass
  stalk
6 garlic cloves
8 spring onions
4cm piece fresh ginger root
3 tablespoons vegetable oil
1 tablespoon coriander seeds
1 teaspoon cumin seeds
½ teaspoon fennel seeds
1 teaspoon shrimp paste (*kapi*)
500ml thin coconut milk (extract)
900g rump steak, sliced
170g green beans
75g sliced bamboo shoots
⅓ sweet red pepper, cut
  into shreds
175ml thick coconut milk
  (cream)
salt
fish sauce (*nam pla*) to taste

serves 6

1 Drain the chillies, remove the stems and scrape out the seeds. Drain the lime leaves.

2 In a food processor or blender, grind the chillies, lime leaves and lemongrass to a paste with the garlic, onions and ginger (add the vegetable oil if necessary). Fry gently for about 12 minutes, stirring frequently to prevent burning.

3 Grind the spices finely in a mortar or spice grinder and add to the pan with the shrimp paste. Cook for 1–2 minutes, then add the thin coconut milk and simmer for 30 minutes until well reduced; a film of oil will be floating on the surface.

4 Cut the beef into narrow strips. Place in the hot curry sauce and add the beans, bamboo shoots and peppers and cook, stirring, until the meat changes colour. Add the thick coconut milk, salt and fish sauce to taste and cook gently until the meat and beans are tender. Serve over rice.

SONGKRAN

THAI OR SOLAR NEW YEAR

The Thai New Year, on April 13, originated from the Indian Holi festival; it is celebrated in the north with more enthusiasm than in other parts of Thailand. The people of Chiang Mai in particular make the Songkran 'water throwing' festival a madcap affair. Three days of high-spirited festivities begin with offerings at the temples and images of the Buddha sprinkled with water, the young showing respect for their elders by bathing their hands in perfumed water. But, formalities dispensed with, the city becomes an aquatic obstacle course for the unwary, a crazy bonanza of water splashing from which no one emerges unscathed. Spices and chilli help to stimulate heat-jaded appetites.

left Songkran, Chang Mai, Alain Evrad/Robert
Harding World Imagery/Getty Images

Yam Neua

BEEF SALAD

This looks wonderful served in 'boats' of hollowed cucumbers, their skins decoratively carved.

225g piece beef fillet
1 teaspoon cracked black pepper
1 teaspoon crushed garlic
1 teaspoon salt
2–3 medium cucumbers
mint leaves to garnish
coriander leaves to garnish

DRESSING
1 lemongrass stalk, finely
  shredded
3 fresh kaffir lime leaves,
  finely shredded
15g fresh coriander leaves
15g fresh small mint leaves
3 garlic cloves, very finely
  chopped
2–6 small 'bird's eye' chillies
2 tablespoons fish sauce
  (*nam pla*)
1½ tablespoons sugar
juice of 1 lime

serves 4-6

1 Rub the surface of the beef with pepper, garlic and salt and place on a rack in an oven dish. Roast at 200°C/400°F/gas 6 for about 10 minutes until the surface is seared but the meat quite underdone inside. Remove from the oven and leave to cool.

2 Mix the shredded lemongrass and lime leaves with the coriander and mint leaves. Combine the garlic, chillies, fish sauce, sugar and lime juice.

3 Very finely shred the beef, toss with the shredded greens and pour on the dressing. Cut the cucumbers in half lengthways and scoop out the seeds. Use a small sharp knife to make decorative patterns on the skin of the cucumbers. Arrange side by side on a platter. Fill with the prepared mixture and chill before serving garnished with mint and coriander.

PLA GOONG

COLD SPICED PRAWNS

24 medium to large
  uncooked prawns
1 medium onion
3 spring onions, chopped
1 tablespoon finely chopped
  lemongrass
2 teaspoons finely shredded
  fresh ginger
1–2 fresh red chillies,
  finely shredded
15g mint leaves
10g coriander leaves
3 lettuce leaves
1 large tomato, cut into wedges
½ small cucumber, deseeded
  and sliced

DRESSING
3 tablespoons lime juice
  (approx. 2 limes)
2 tablespoons fish sauce
  (*nam pla*)
1½ tablespoons palm sugar,
  crumbled
3 garlic cloves, finely chopped
1 tablespoon roasted peanuts,
  finely chopped

serves 6

1 Peel the prawns, leaving the tails on. Make a deep incision down the centre back of each prawn and pull away the dark vein. Rinse and drain. Bring a saucepan of lightly salted water to the boil, add the prawns and boil for about 1 minute, drain and leave to cool.

2 Peel the onion and slice thinly from top to base to make narrow, curved pieces. In a bowl, combine both sorts of onion, the lemongrass, ginger, chillies and herbs, add the prawns and toss to combine evenly. Place the washed and dried lettuce on a serving plate and arrange the prawn salad on top.

3 In a screwtop jar combine the lime juice, fish sauce, sugar, garlic and peanuts. Close and shake vigorously until the sugar has dissolved. Pour over the salad and garnish with tomato and cucumber.

LAAB NEUA

RAW BEEF WITH CHILLI AND MINT

2 tablespoons short-grain
  white rice
1–3 dried red chillies
400g raw beef
  (rump or round)
3 tablespoons fish sauce
  (*nam pla*)
75ml lime juice
3 teaspoons palm sugar
3 teaspoons finely shredded
  fresh ginger
30g spring onions,
  finely shredded
55g red salad onions,
  finely chopped
½ sweet red pepper, shredded
15g mint leaves
lettuce leaves

serves 6

1 Place the rice in a dry saucepan and cook slowly to a rich golden brown. Remove to a blender or mortar and grind to a coarse powder. Similarly toast the chillies, remove stems and shake out seeds. Grind into flakes.

2 Using a cleaver or a food mincer, mince (grind) the beef coarsely and mix with the rice and chilli. Combine the fish sauce, lime juice, sugar and ginger and stir into the beef, mixing well. Chill for 30 minutes while the flavours develop. Mix in the onions, pepper and half the mint leaves, coarsely shredded. Pile into lettuce cups and garnish with the remaining mint.

The Festive Food of Thailand

Som Tam

PAPAYA SALAD

1 unripe or very firm papaya,
   peeled
1 large carrot, peeled
1 small onion, peeled
1 green chilli, seeded
lettuce leaves

DRESSING
juice of 2 large limes
2 tablespoons fish sauce
   (*nam pla*)
brown sugar to taste
salt
white pepper

serves 4-6

1 Very finely grate the papaya, carrot and onion. Mince or finely shred the chilli.

2 Combine the lime juice, fish sauce, sugar, salt and pepper to make a tart dressing with a hint of sweetness. Pour over the salad and chill. To serve, arrange the salad in a dish lined with lettuce leaves.

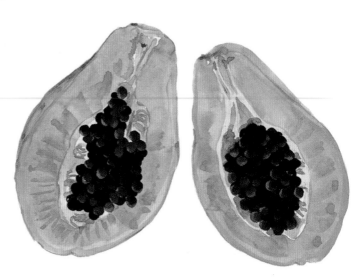

right Shaun Egan/The
Image Bank/Getty Images

The Festive Food of Thailand

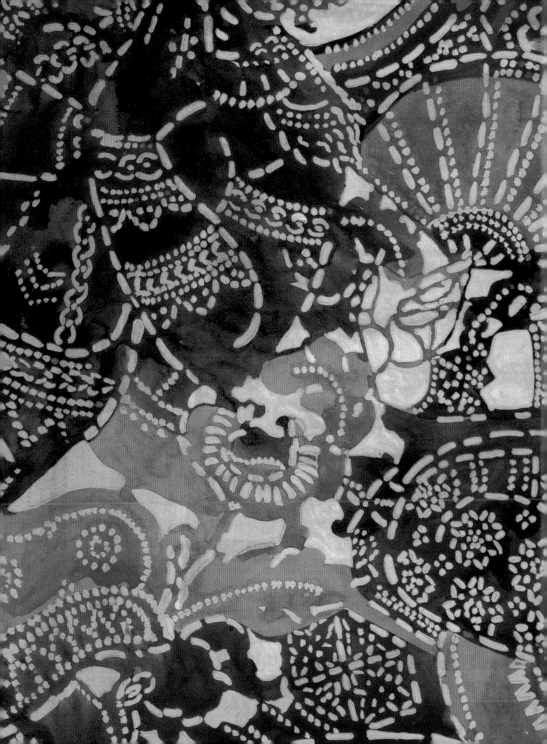